# WHAT WOULD HAPPEN IF...

# ALL THE FOSSIL FUELS RAN OUT?

Written by Izzi Howell

Illustrated by Paula Bossio

WORLD BOOK

www.worldbook.com

# READING TIPS

This book asks readers to ponder the question *what would happen if all the fossil fuels ran out?* Readers will discover why we use so much fossil fuel, why supplies are beginning to run low, and what other forms of energy we can use instead of fossil fuels. Use these tips to help readers consider the ripple effects of certain actions and events.

## Before Reading

Explain to readers that this book uses cause and effect to show how human activity can affect the environment, living things, and our planet's resources. Cause and effect can help us think about why things happen the way they do. It can also help us think about what might happen in the future because of our actions and choices today. Encourage readers to be on the lookout for examples of a cause and effect structure as they explore what would happen if all the fossil fuels ran out.

## During Reading

Discuss with readers how some actions and events have multiple causes and others have multiple effects. Explain that it can be tricky to keep all the if/then scenarios straight in our minds, so it can be helpful to create a visual guide. Encourage readers to draw and add notes to their own cause and effect maps like those found on pages 8-9, 26-27, and 36-37.

## After Reading

After finishing the book, discuss with readers how their understandings and opinions of fossil fuels and their impact on our environment have changed. Additionally, you can have readers respond to the comprehension questions included on page 46 and complete the Chain of Events activity on page 47 to further extend the learning.

Visit **www.worldbook.com/resources** for additional, free educational materials.

There is a glossary of terms on pages 44–45. Terms defined in the glossary are in boldface type that **looks like this** on their first appearance on any spread (two facing pages).

# Contents

# Fueling our world

**Fossil fuels** make the world go around! These fuels (coal, natural gas, and oil) power the vehicles we drive, provide electricity and heat to buildings, and are used to make such materials as plastic. It's hardly surprising that we use a huge amount of these handy resources every year.

Gasoline is made from oil.

But unfortunately, we don't have an everlasting supply of fossil fuels. They are **nonrenewable** resources, which means that once they're gone ... they're gone forever! Ever since the late 1700's, we've been using huge amounts of fossil fuels. Now, our supplies are starting to run low. Scientists predict that if we continue to use fossil fuels at the same rate, it won't be long before we use them all up.

We depend so heavily on fossil fuels that it's hard to imagine a world without them. However, like it or not, we will eventually run out if we continue to use them. It's time to start using other forms of energy before it's too late!

DID YOU KNOW?

More than 80 percent of the world's energy comes from fossil fuels.

Nearly three-quarters of **greenhouse gas emissions** from human activity over the past 20 years are from burning fossil fuels.

Places that are rich in coal today were once swampy forest areas. These prehistoric plants and trees became the coal we use today!

Coal is the world's greatest source of energy for generating electricity.

Fossil fuels have been used since ancient times, but we use far more today than ever before.

## THINK ABOUT IT!

Why do you think we use more fossil fuels now than in the past?

How about an apple instead?

# Fossil fuel frenzy

When you fill up your car at the gas station, did you know that the gasoline you pump could have once been a dinosaur?! Gasoline, like all **fossil fuels,** is made from the **decomposed** remains of living things that died millions of years ago. That includes plants, animals, and yes, dinosaurs!

When prehistoric living things died, their remains were eventually buried under layers of sand and mud. Over time, the weight of these layers pressed down on the remains. The resulting pressure and heat, along with other natural processes, turned the remains into fossil fuels.

**FUN FACT!**

Fossil fuels get their name from the fact that they are made from the remains of ancient living things, just like fossils!

Hey fossil!

Hey fossil!

This coal mine is open on the surface. Coal mines can also be found deep underground.

We dig coal out of the ground in mines. In the past, this was done by hand, but today it is mostly done by machines. Oil and natural gas are **extracted** from deep underground using large pumps.

Oil and natural gas are pumped from underneath the seabed on offshore platforms.

DID YOU KNOW?

Although some dinosaur remains have been turned into fossil fuels, the vast majority of animal remains that became fossil fuels were from teeny tiny plankton!

# FOSSIL FUEL FRENZY

**Fossil fuels** have many uses.
Let's take a look!

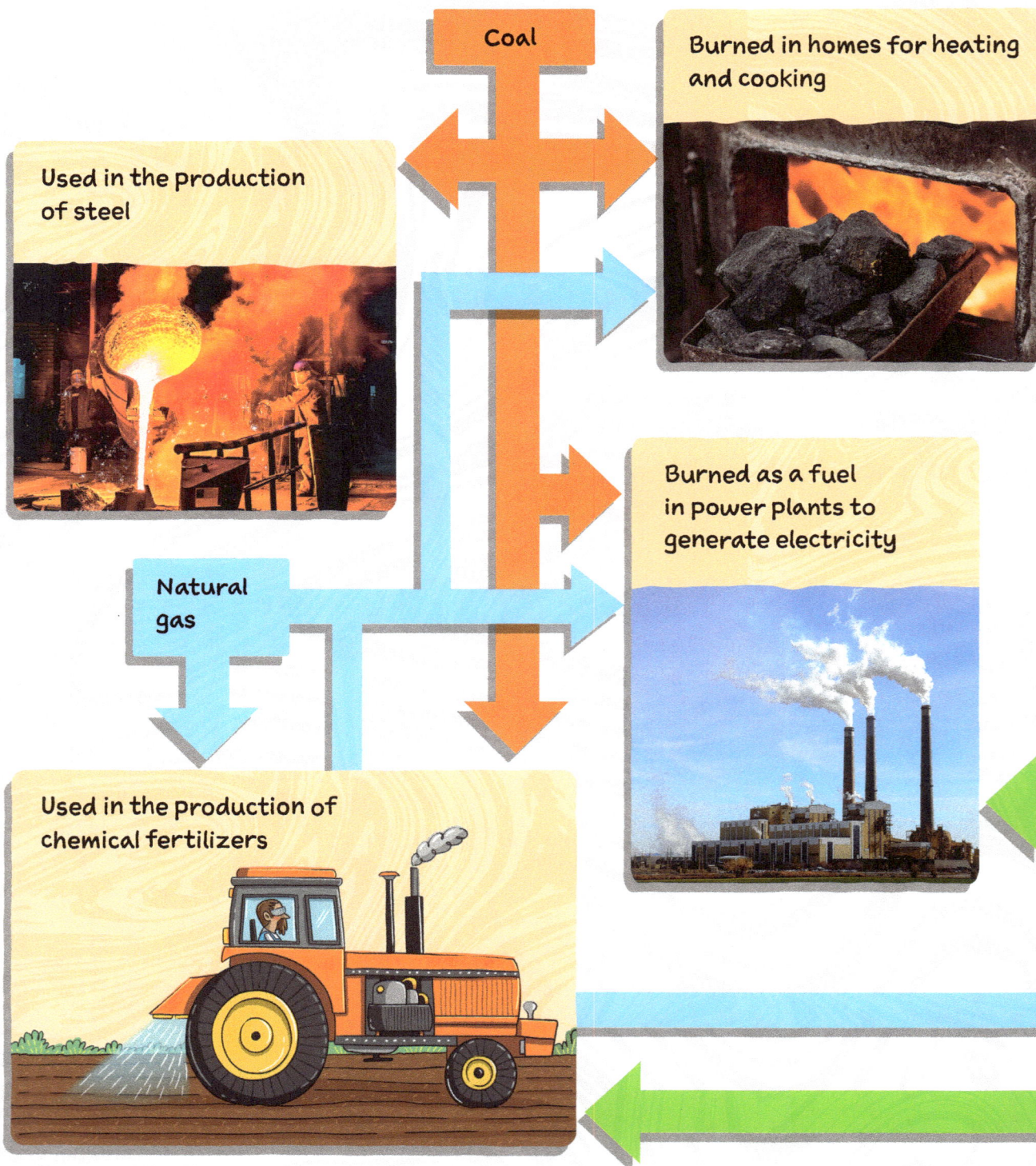

Coal

Burned in homes for heating and cooking

Used in the production of steel

Natural gas

Burned as a fuel in power plants to generate electricity

Used in the production of chemical fertilizers

Oil

Turned into fuel for vehicles, such as gasoline, diesel, kerosene, and jet fuel

Turned into household products, such as toiletries, clothing, glue, and cleaners

Used to make plastic

## THINK ABOUT IT!

How many items in your home are powered by or made of fossil fuels?

9

## FOSSIL FUEL FRENZY

Because **fossil fuels** take so long to form, they are considered to be **nonrenewable** resources. Technically, more fossil fuels will form over time from the remains of other living things, but they won't be ready to use for millions of years. So once we've used up our supply of fossil fuels, that's it for a very, very long time!

So how long do we have left?

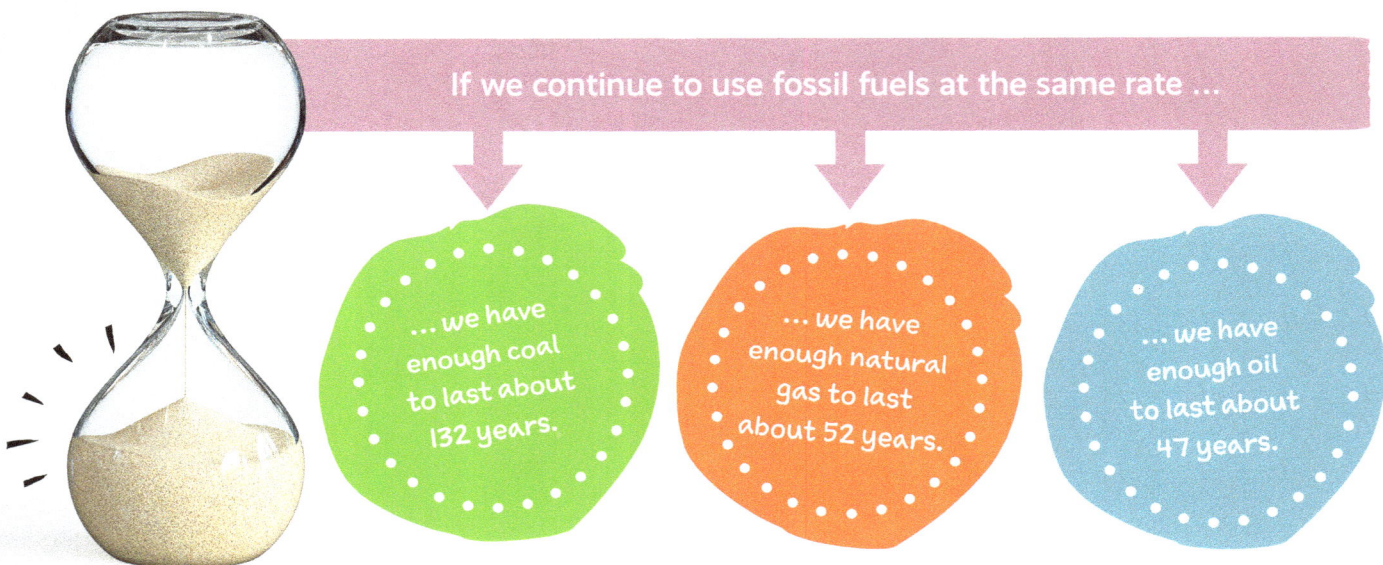

If we continue to use fossil fuels at the same rate ...

...we have enough coal to last about 132 years.

...we have enough natural gas to last about 52 years.

...we have enough oil to last about 47 years.

This means that the children of today will witness the end of natural gas and oil during their lifetimes. Their grandchildren and great-grandchildren will be around when coal finally runs out. The end of fossil fuels isn't something for us to ignore and leave for distant future generations. It's happening, and it's happening soon!

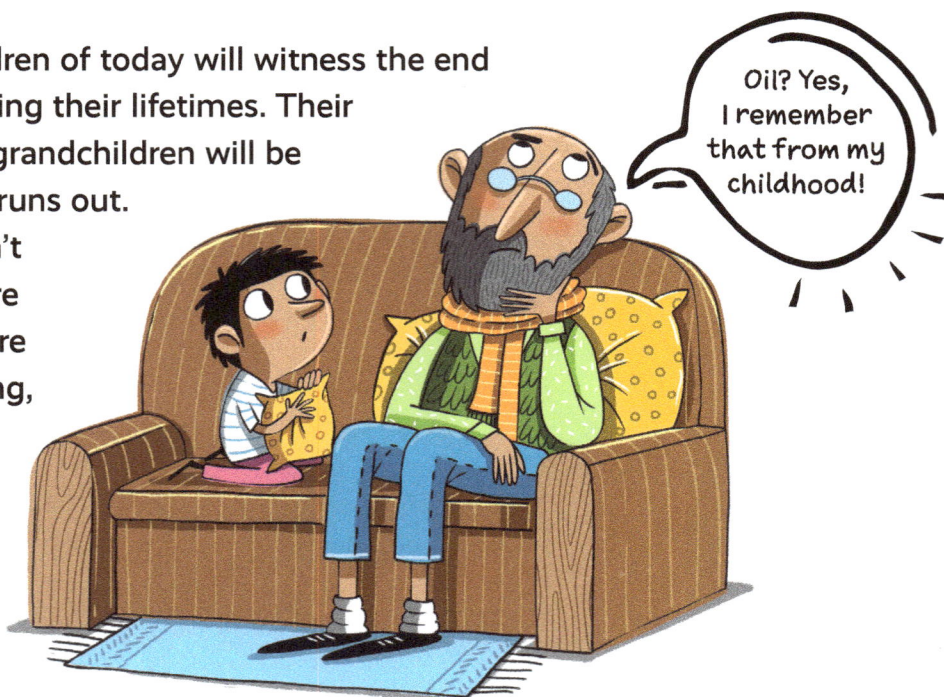

Oil? Yes, I remember that from my childhood!

**END FOSSIL FUELS NOW**

Protesters call for the end of fossil fuels now to avoid further damage to our planet.

However, the business of fossil fuels is huge, because they are such widely used resources. Some companies and even a few countries have even become very rich by **extracting** and selling fossil fuels. Even though we have evidence that stocks of fossil fuels are running low (and that they are destroying our planet—see pages 12–15!), many businesses are spending a lot of money trying to convince governments and people that we should continue using fossil fuels.

**THINK ABOUT IT!**

Why do you think fossil fuel companies want us to continue using fossil fuels as normal?

**DID YOU KNOW?**

In 2022, the company in charge of oil in Saudi Arabia made $161 billion in profit!

# Climate complications

Many scientists currently recommend that we should transition to other energy sources as soon as possible, rather than waiting for **fossil fuels** to run out. This is because our heavy use of fossil fuels is creating a climate crisis.

When fossil fuels are burned, they release a large amount of **carbon dioxide** and other **greenhouse gases.** These gases gather in the **atmosphere** and trap heat from the sun close to Earth's surface. This is known as the **greenhouse effect.** This effect increases the surface temperature on Earth (also known as **global warming**).

Many natural **habitats** are changing as a result of global warming. Ice sheets and glaciers are melting at the poles. Sea levels are rising around the world, flooding many coastal areas. Green, leafy areas are being destroyed by heat waves and are turning into desert.

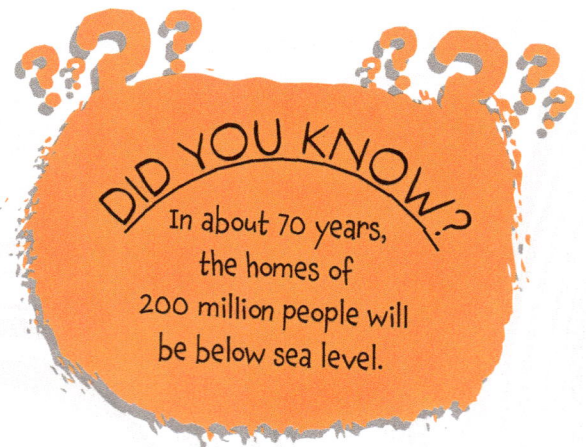

**DID YOU KNOW?**
In about 70 years, the homes of 200 million people will be below sea level.

Global warming changes our climate. It has led to an increase in more extreme weather events, such as storms, flooding, and **droughts.** These events can have a devastating impact on all living things.

Burning fossil fuels also creates air pollution. Power plants and vehicles release **toxic** gases and tiny particles that we can easily breathe in. These particles are small enough to get into our bloodstream, and they can cause breathing problems or even such diseases as cancer.

## THINK ABOUT IT!

Have you recently experienced any unusual weather where you live?

13

So, if we stop using **fossil fuels,** problem solved, right? Unfortunately not. Many scientists are worried about climate tipping points that will lead to major, often irreversible changes to the environment. The rise in Earth's temperature due to **global warming** has pushed us ever closer to several disastrous tipping points, including the melting of important ice sheets and the destruction of tropical coral reefs.

DID YOU KNOW?
The ice sheets in Greenland and Antarctica are losing more than three times as much ice every year than they were 30 years ago.

Coral reefs are under threat because oceans are absorbing the extra **carbon dioxide** in the **atmosphere,** which makes their water more acidic. Coral can't grow properly in acidic water.

## CLIMATE COMPLICATIONS

If these ecosystems are lost, stopping the use of fossil fuels won't be enough to bring them back. Restoring them will be a very complicated, long process, which may not even work in the end. However, if we transition away from fossil fuels now, we are less likely to reach these tipping points and so will have much less damage to undo later.

The loss of the Amazon rain forest due to **drought, deforestation,** and **wildfires** would be another climate tipping point.

Hi! I'm Steve Pye, a British scientist who studies energy and our climate. Fossil fuels have already done a huge amount of damage to our planet. In my research, I use computer programs to predict how our climate will be affected if we continue to use them. Around 60 percent of oil and natural gas reserves and 90 percent of our remaining coal must remain underground if we are to prevent a climate catastrophe.

# Running low

If we don't listen to scientists and continue to use **fossil fuels** as normal, our supplies will eventually start to run low. People will start to go to more extreme lengths to get their hands on fossil fuels.

In some areas, such techniques as **fracking** have already been introduced. Fracking is a way of releasing natural gas and oil that are trapped underground inside rock and would otherwise be impossible to **extract**. Huge holes are drilled into the ground, and water, sand, and chemicals are injected into the rock at high pressure. This forces natural gas and oil out of the rock.

A fracking site in the United States. Excess natural gas that can't be collected is burned—can you spot the flame?

Fracking is pretty controversial, because it can create a lot of problems. Drilling into the rock can trigger small earthquakes in the area around the site. It also uses and pollutes a huge amount of water, which isn't particularly good for the environment!

Water from a lake is pumped out to use for fracking. There will be now be less water available for farms or for the local water supply.

Hi! I'm Tim Baxter, an Australian energy scientist. My colleagues and I are very concerned about the introduction of fracking in many countries around the world. Not only does it contribute to **climate change**, it also puts the people and wild **habitats** surrounding the fracking site at great risk. We've even started seeing more cases of certain serious health problems around fracking sites, due to pollution from the **toxic** chemicals used. Our job is to spread the word about our findings and hope that people listen!

As well as introducing such new techniques as **fracking, fossil fuel** companies have also started looking for new areas where fossil fuels may be hidden away. Their target? Protected natural spaces that are supposed to be left alone because of the special **habitats,** plants, and animals found there!

The Arctic is believed to hold nearly 25 percent of Earth's undiscovered oil and gas supply.

Many of these places are in less economically developed countries where governments want to boost their economies and reduce poverty. It's hard for them to refuse money from rich and powerful fossil fuel companies. More economically developed countries are also allowing this to happen. They are worried about fossil fuel supplies running low.

DID YOU KNOW?
Fossil fuels are already being **extracted** from or plan to be taken from more than 3,000 protected sites around the world.

Extracting fossil fuels will do huge amounts of damage to these unique wild areas. Habitats will be cut down to create space for mines, pumps, and roads to transport resources. Animals and plants will be poisoned by spilled oil or chemicals used to extract the fuels.

This sticky black mess is spilled oil from an oil pump in the Amazon rain forest. Oil is very hard to clean up and will poison and hurt many rain forest animals.

Some people believe that fracking and extracting fossil fuels from protected areas are justifiable. Without them, we are at risk of running out of fossil fuels needed for important services, such as transportation, heating, and cooking.

Others think that investing in these techniques is only delaying the inevitable. Although these methods will provide us with more fossil fuels in the short run, they don't do anything to solve the long-term issue. They are also hugely damaging to the environment. Plus, let's not forget that extracting more fossil fuels is only going to make our climate crisis worse!

## THINK ABOUT IT!

What do you think about these methods of extracting fossil fuels? Are they worth it?

# The end

As we get closer to the end of our **fossil fuel** reserves, coal, oil, and natural gas will become much harder to come by. What will life look like as we run out of these valuable fuels?

The first big change we'll notice is that fossil fuel companies will start to raise the price of fuel. Heating and powering our homes and buying gasoline for our cars will become much more expensive. This will cause many problems for people. Some people will be forced to choose between food and other basic supplies, gasoline, and heat and power in their home.

Eventually, there won't be enough fossil fuels to go around. Governments will have to decide how to **ration** the coal, oil, and natural gas that remains. For example, gasoline may be reserved for emergency service vehicles, such as ambulances and fire trucks. Factories, hospitals, and supermarkets may be allowed to use more electricity than homes and other businesses.

All of the machines in hospitals require lots of electricity.

# THINK ABOUT IT!

If you had to ration fossil fuels, how would you divide them up?

Many people around the world will experience **blackouts** with no access to electricity or heating. This will be very inconvenient or even dangerous. There won't be any electricity to power refrigerators, ovens, phones, or other everyday appliances. There will be no heating in the winter or air conditioning in the summer.

## DID YOU KNOW?

Blackouts already happen from time to time. They can be caused by a natural disaster that destroys power cables or if there's more demand for electricity than can be supplied.

Eventually, the day will come when no **fossil fuels** remain on Earth. With no fuel and limited electricity from existing green energy sources, the world would quickly grind to a halt.

Travel will become extremely difficult without gasoline for cars, buses, and planes. People will become stuck in their local area. We won't be able to transport food or goods across countries or around the world. This will greatly affect our food supply.

Without gasoline for cars, the roads will be very empty—perfect for bicycling!

THE END

That's not the only problem affecting our food. Farmers won't be able to get fuel to power tractors or farm equipment, or electricity to power key machines, such as those used to milk cows. And even if farmers were able to harvest **crops** and transport them to factories, there wouldn't be any electricity to run the machines that process ingredients.

This wheat could be picked by hand, but it's much MUCH faster with a combine harvester!

## THINK ABOUT IT!

Many of the foods we eat every day, such as oil, bread, and noodles, are made in factories. What do you think it would be like if you had to make them by hand?

And it's not just food factories—no factory would be able to produce goods without electricity. As a result, many people would lose their jobs and wouldn't have any money to support themselves.

23

With the world in crisis, there'll be a huge rush to find ways to help us live normally again. First, we'll need more electricity, and fast! Wind **turbines,** solar panels, hydroelectric dams, and nuclear power plants (see pages 32–37) could be built around the world to generate electricity.

However, these machines are massive and complex and are not quick to assemble. And if we didn't have any electricity to power factories to produce new parts or fuel to transport equipment, this would take even longer.

Normal cars and vans could be swapped for electric cars, powered with electricity from **renewable** sources. Electric trains could provide useful public transportation within cities and across countries. Prototypes for solar-powered planes and electric cargo ships are currently being tested and would hopefully be ready in time to carry people and goods across the planet.

Check it out – a solar-powered plane!

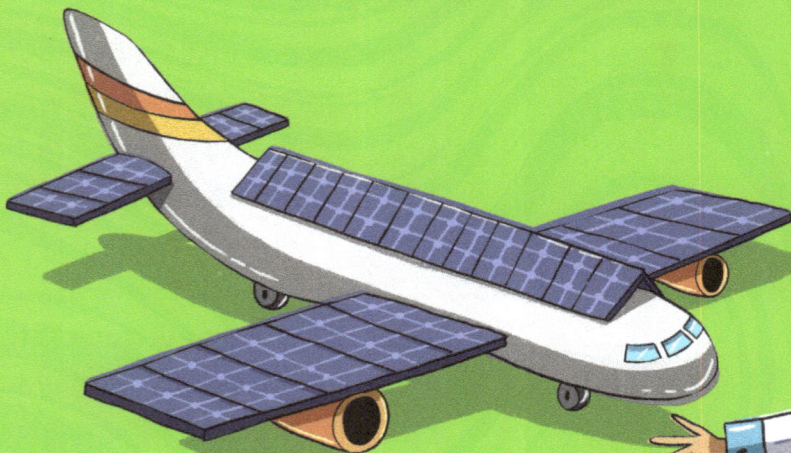

But wait ... what about plastic? Luckily, there are ways of making plastics without **extracting** new **fossil fuels.** First of all, we can recycle existing plastic into new plastic items (which as a bonus also reduces plastic pollution!). Scientists have also developed some bioplastics, which are made from renewable materials, such as plants, and can fully **biodegrade.**

Many grocery stores are already offering bioplastic bags for produce.

Hi! I'm Eugene Chen. I'm a chemist with a particular interest in **sustainability.** My team and I have been researching alternatives to plastic and have come up with a new design for a type of bioplastic called PHA. This bioplastic is made from a renewable material you probably have at home—sugar! Objects made from PHA biodegrade quickly in any environment, so they leave no trace.

## FUN FACT!

It takes up to 200 years for a straw made of traditional plastic to biodegrade in the ocean. A straw made of PHA takes just 180 days and leaves no dangerous **microplastics!**

25

## THE END

Running out of **fossil fuels** will create a massive global crisis that will affect every aspect of our lives. Things will be very hard and difficult while we adjust to the new circumstances. However, all is not lost! There are many great solutions to this problem, such as **renewable** sources of energy, which will help us get back to normal. Let's see how …

Plastics would be replaced by bioplastics made from renewable materials.

What would happen as fossil fuels ran low … and then ran out?

When gasoline runs out, we'd only be able to use vehicles that require no fuel, such as bicycles. Global transportation and travel will become almost impossible.

Gasoline would become very expensive or reserved for priority vehicles, such as ambulances.

Over time, we would switch to electric cars and other small vehicles (and hopefully large vehicles, too!). People could travel long distance on electric trains and ships, and solar-powered planes.

Prices for electricity and heating would rise sky-high. **Blackouts** would become regular occurrences, because there wouldn't be enough power to go around.

Eventually, we'd be left with very limited electricity to power homes, factories, farms, and many other essential services. This would be a global crisis.

New solar panels, wind **turbines**, hydroelectric dams, and nuclear power plants would be built to generate electricity.

## THINK ABOUT IT!

What would your life be like without fossil fuels? Do you think it would be better, worse, or the same as your life now?

# Silver linings

Running out of **fossil fuels** would be bad news for travel, the economy, and pretty much most aspects of human life, but extremely good news for the environment!

So far, serious environmental warnings from scientists haven't been enough to convince people that they need to reduce their use of fossil fuels. Using up every last bit of fossil fuel on Earth may be the only way to make them stop.

With no more fossil fuels left to burn on Earth, we wouldn't be able to add any more **greenhouse gases** into our **atmosphere,** so our climate crisis wouldn't get any worse. However, the years of burning fossil fuels that led up to this point would have left our climate in a terrible state. We'd have to do a huge amount of work to fix the damage done.

Ok, fine, I'll stop!

Luckily, there are some ways to remove **carbon dioxide** from our atmosphere and store it, so that it doesn't contribute to the **greenhouse effect.** One of the easiest and most effective techniques is planting trees. Trees remove carbon dioxide from the atmosphere as part of **photosynthesis.** The carbon dioxide is stored in the tree as long as it stays alive.

Planting more trees now will help slow down the amount of carbon dioxide being added to our atmosphere.

Yum, delicious carbon dioxide!

**FUN FACT!**

A mature tree absorbs about 50 pounds (22 kilograms) of carbon dioxide from the atmosphere every year!

We can also use technology to remove carbon from the atmosphere. Direct air capture uses large fans to push air through filters that remove carbon dioxide. This carbon dioxide can then be used to make fuel, concrete, or even carbonated soda!

The carbon dioxide collected by these direct air capture fans in Switzerland is used by a local greenhouse (in the background) to help its cucumbers grow better!

Once **fossil fuels** run out, we won't be able to produce any more traditional plastic, which means that we won't have any additional plastic pollution. However, there's still the problem of what to do with all the plastic we've been dumping for years and years!

Most plastic takes hundreds of years to **decompose,** so we'll be dealing with plastic garbage long after the end of fossil fuels. When left to break down in water or in the soil, plastic can break down into tiny particles called **microplastics,** which can pass into the bodies of living things and cause harm.

## THINK ABOUT IT!

What do you do with plastic items once you've finished with them? Where do you think they end up?

## DID YOU KNOW?

Experts believe that there are already 83 to 220 million tons (75 to 199 million tonnes) of plastic in our oceans.

After the end of plastic (and ideally long before), we'll need to clean up all the plastic waste properly. Some can be recycled into new plastic products, which will be in high demand once new plastic can't be produced. Scientists are also working on other ways to safely dispose of plastic, including using tiny plastic-munching bacteria to break it down!

Although there will be some strategies to help undo the damage to our environment, healing our planet will be very slow and far from perfect. Continuing to burn fossil fuels until they are used up will damage the environment to such an extent that it may never be able to fully return to how it was before.

However, it's important to remember that Earth has been through many major changes throughout its history. Temperatures have been higher, lower, and somewhere in between. So far, life has always found a way to survive! It may be a slow and difficult process, but eventually our planet will reach a new normal.

I'm back!

# Act now

It's clear that continuing to use **fossil fuels** as we have been is only going to end in huge amounts of damage to our environment and total chaos when we run out. Luckily, it isn't too late to take action to prevent these disasters.

Fossil fuels aren't our only energy options. There are many other alternative energy sources that we can use instead, including solar energy, hydroelectric energy, wind energy, and nuclear energy. Let's find out more!

Energy for you and you and you!

Solar panels can provide energy directly to homes and businesses!

FUN FACT! In one hour, Earth receives enough energy from the sun to provide power for an entire year!

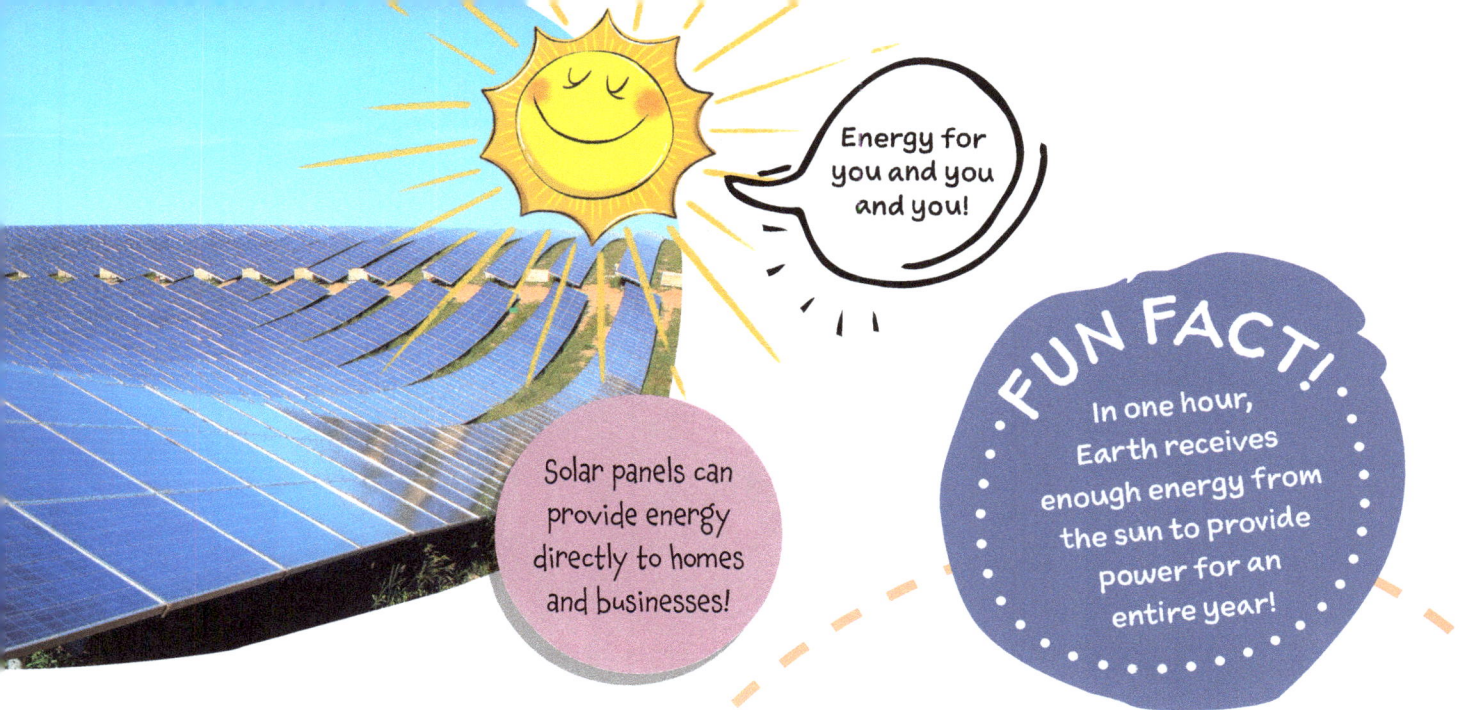

Did you know that the sun already provides a huge amount of our planet's power? Most plants use light energy from the sun to make food for themselves (a process known as **photosynthesis**). These plants provide energy for animals in the form of food!

But sunlight can also be used to generate electricity. This is usually done via large solar panels filled with incredible devices known as photovoltaic cells, which can turn sunlight straight into electricity! Solar panels can be placed on the roof of a building to provide it with its own electricity or grouped together in huge solar farms in sunny places to provide electricity for a town or city.

Hi! I'm Ali Hajimiri, an Iranian American electrical engineer. Solar panels on Earth's surface are an excellent way of generating electricity, but they don't work so well on a cloudy day or at night. So I'm working on a project to see if we can gather solar power from space! Up there, we can generate solar power 24/7 from huge solar panels mounted on satellites. This electricity could then be beamed back down to Earth.

33

Hydroelectric energy comes from the power of moving water. It is usually generated in a hydroelectric dam built across a river. As water rushes through the dam, it spins the blades of **turbines** inside, which generate electricity.

**FUN FACT!** At full capacity, the Three Gorges Dam in China can generate enough electricity in one day to power more than 5 million homes for a month!

It's hard to see the turbines inside a dam—wind turbines are much easier to spot! The movement of the wind pushes the blades of a wind turbine, which are connected to a rotor that generates electricity.

Wind turbines are often built at sea. Winds are much higher away from shore, which means that more electricity can be generated!

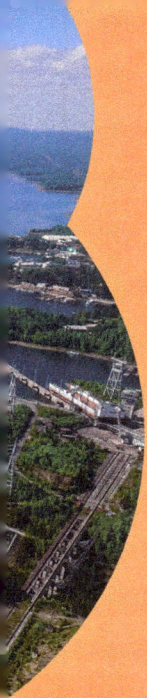

Nuclear energy comes from powerful changes in the core of **atoms.** This creates a huge amount of heat that can be used to make steam. The steam, in turn, can be used to drive machines that generate electric power. Engineers have built devices called nuclear reactors to produce and control nuclear energy in nuclear power plants.

This may look like a **fossil fuel** power plant, but it's actually powered by nuclear energy! The tall towers are for cooling down steam and releasing heat that isn't needed.

DID YOU KNOW?

That's not all! There are many other ways of generating energy without the use of fossil fuels, including geothermal energy (using natural heat from underground) and tidal energy (generated by movement of the tides).

I don't think that's how it works!'

## ACT NOW

Solar, wind, hydroelectric, and nuclear energy are all great alternatives to **fossil fuels** because they don't release any **greenhouse gases.** Solar, wind, and hydroelectric energy are also **renewable** forms of energy, so we'll never run out. However, these forms of generating energy do also have some disadvantages.

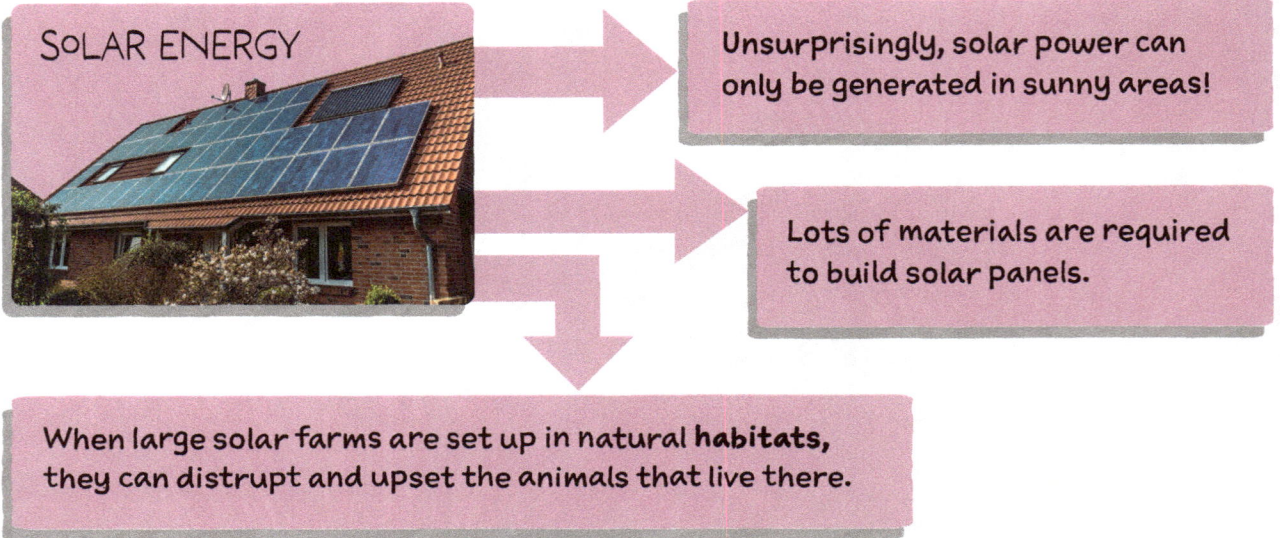

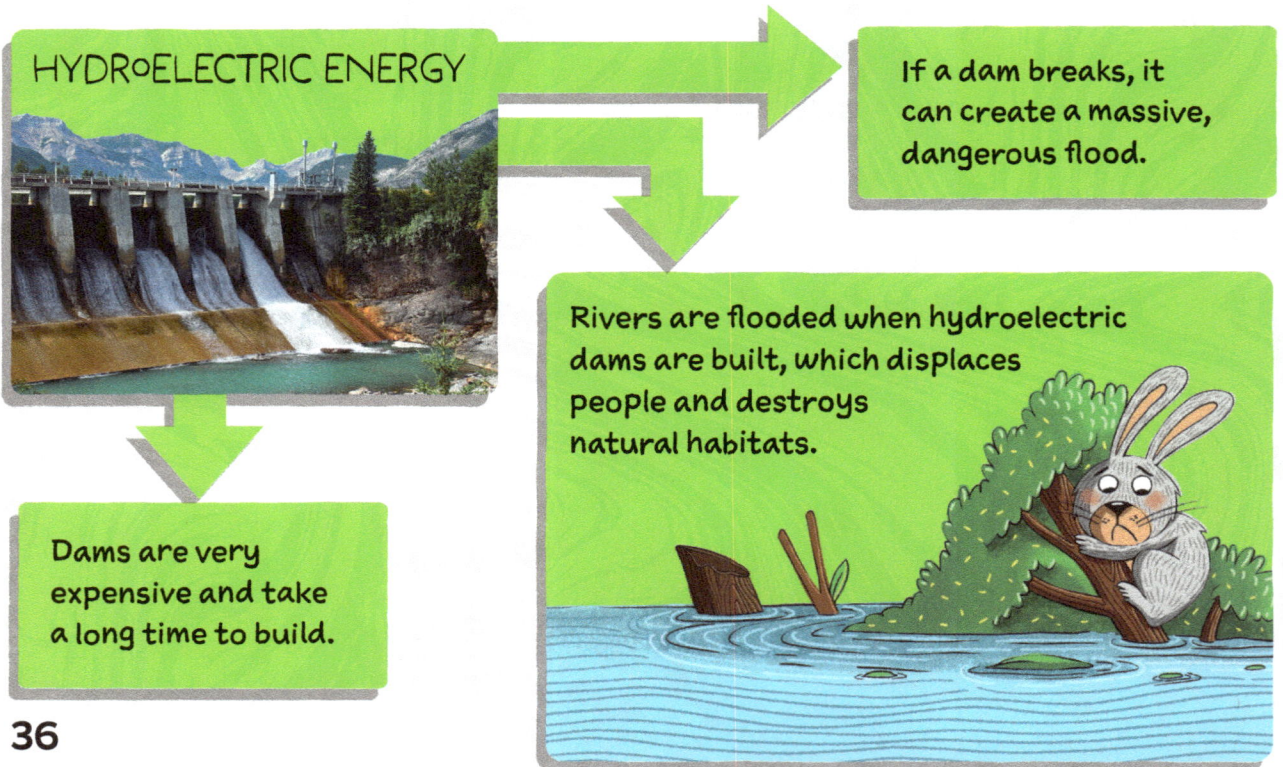

### SOLAR ENERGY

Unsurprisingly, solar power can only be generated in sunny areas!

Lots of materials are required to build solar panels.

When large solar farms are set up in natural **habitats,** they can distrupt and upset the animals that live there.

### HYDROELECTRIC ENERGY

If a dam breaks, it can create a massive, dangerous flood.

Rivers are flooded when hydroelectric dams are built, which displaces people and destroys natural habitats.

Dams are very expensive and take a long time to build.

Birds, insects, and bats can be hurt or killed if they fly into a wind **turbine**.

Not again!

## WIND ENERGY

Electricity is only produced when the wind blows!

Wind turbines can be noisy.

## NUCLEAR ENERGY

Nuclear waste is **radioactive** and very hard and expensive to dispose of safely.

In the event of an accident, many people and living things in the surrounding area would be poisoned or killed.

It's clear that there is no perfect energy source. However, most people agree that the benefits to these types of energy outweigh the disadvantages. And even if they didn't, they'll eventually be our only option once fossil fuels run out!

## THINK ABOUT IT!

Which method of generating energy would work well where you live?

## ACT NOW

The best solution to the **fossil fuel** crisis would be to hugely reduce our use of coal, natural gas, and oil before they run out. Many countries have already changed over to alternative forms of energy—now it's time for the rest of the planet to follow suit. If we build new solar farms, hydroelectric dams, wind **turbines,** and nuclear power plants now, we'll be able to slowly transition away from fossil fuels and leave the remaining supplies in the ground. In this way, we'll avoid a global crisis and keep **climate change** from getting worse.

The giant parts of a new wind turbine are lifted into place by crane.

**FUN FACT!**

The blades of the world's largest wind turbine are 420 feet (128 meters) long!

Governments and politicians are responsible for making these big decisions and changes to our energy systems. However, there are also things that everyone can do to make a difference! For example, you could switch over to an energy provider that generates its electricity without the use of fossil fuels.

Why not try to reduce your own energy consumption? Use public transportation, bike, or walk instead of driving a car powered by gasoline. Be more energy efficient at home by turning off lights and appliances when they're not in use, or hang clothes out to dry instead of using a dryer.

Electric cars run on electricity instead of gasoline, which means that they don't release any air pollution or **greenhouse gases** as exhaust. However, don't forget that the electricity used to power the car may come from burning greenhouse gases!

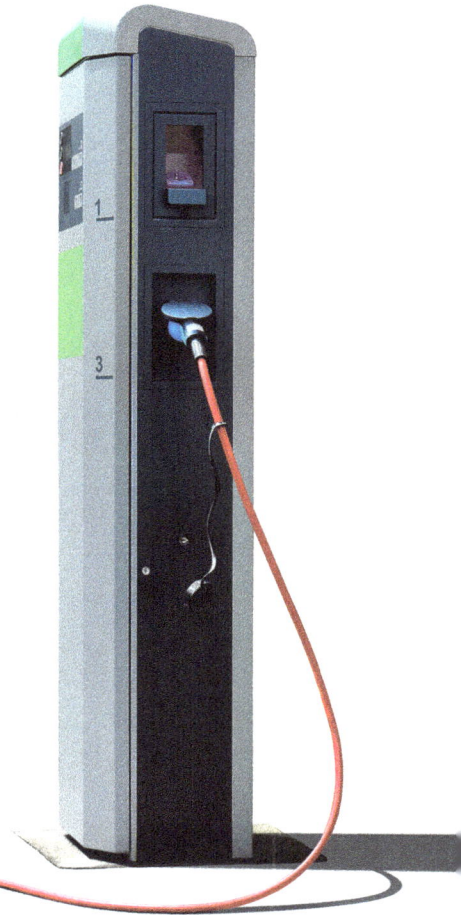

## THINK ABOUT IT!

How much energy do you use every day? How could you make your life more energy efficient?

# Conclusion

Tick tock! The clock is ticking for our remaining supplies of **fossil fuels.** But what to do? Many scientists believe we should leave them in the ground. Fossil fuel companies want to keep **extracting** them and selling them. Lots of people are worried about how the end of fossil fuels will affect their day-to-day lives but aren't sure what to do.

Try to reduce your use of fossil fuels through small changes, such as using reusable fabric grocery bags instead of paper or plastic bags.

We can't put off a decision for much longer. Time is running out, and if we don't act soon, we'll use up our remaining supplies without having a backup plan in place.

## FUN FACT!

More than 100 cities around the world already get at least 70 percent of their energy from **renewable** sources.

If we start now, we have plenty of time to start building new energy sources, such as this solar thermal power plant, so that we can generate all our energy without using fossil fuels.

What's this black sticky stuff?

Whatever happens, fossil fuels won't be gone forever. Millions of years from now, fossil fuels will regenerate on Earth once more. Let's hope that whoever lives on our planet then will use them more sensibly and sustainably!

# Summary

So, exactly what would happen if **fossil fuels** ran out? Check your understanding of the information in this book.

Present day

We gradually transition away from fossil fuels by making such changes as switching to **renewable** sources of energy.

We continue to use up our remaining supplies of fossil fuels.

We run out of fossil fuels.

Where has it all gone?!

Renewable sources of energy will provide us with electricity for many, many years to come (and they won't destroy our planet!).

Levels of **greenhouse gases** in our **atmosphere** won't get worse, and **global warming** and **climate change** will stay the same. We can then work on removing carbon from our atmosphere and undoing the damage to our planet.

More and more greenhouse gases will be released into the atmosphere, making climate change and global warming even worse. We may eventually do so much damage to our planet that it won't be able to recover.

We switch to electric vehicles.

There aren't any fuels to power vehicles. Travel and transportation will come to a standstill.

We can recycle existing plastics and create new bioplastics from renewable materials.

We won't be able to produce any more plastic.

With no fossil fuels to burn to generate electricity, we will experience a terrible global electricity shortage.

## THINK ABOUT IT!

What do you think will happen with fossil fuels in your lifetime? What do you hope will happen?

Eventually, we will build new renewable forms of energy, but this will take some time.

# Glossary

**atmosphere**—the blanket of gases that surrounds Earth, including nitrogen and oxygen, plus smaller amounts of such gases as carbon dioxide

**atom**—the tiniest unit of any element

**biodegrade**—to decay naturally without doing harm to the environment

**blackout**—a period with no electricity or lights

**carbon dioxide**—a gas absorbed by plants that can contribute to global warming

**climate change**—changes in the world's weather, in particular an increase in temperature, which scientists believe are mainly due to human activity

**crop**—a plant grown for food, such as apples, carrots, or potatoes

**decompose**—to decay and break down into smaller parts

**deforestation**—the cutting down of trees and forests by people

**drought**—a long period with little or no rain

**emission**—a release, such as giving off gas

**extract**—to remove

Hey fossil!

Hey fossil!

**fossil fuel**—a fuel such as natural gas, oil, or coal that was formed over millions of years from the remains of animals and plants

**fracking**—cracking underground rock to extract oil and natural gas from it

**global warming**—an increase in temperatures on Earth due to the greenhouse effect

**greenhouse effect**—the effect caused by greenhouse gases (see below!)

**greenhouse gas**—a gas such as carbon dioxide or methane that gathers in the atmosphere and traps heat from the sun close to Earth's surface

**habitat**—the place where an animal or plant usually lives

**microplastic**—a very tiny piece of plastic

**nonrenewable**—something that can only be used once and can't be replaced

**photosynthesis**—the process by which plants make their own food using sunlight

**radioactive**—extremely harmful because it contains dangerous energy from the breaking up of atoms (watch out!)

**ration**—to limit the amount of something that someone can have

**renewable**—something that can be used again and again and will never run out

**sustainability**—doing things that are able to continue over a long period of time because they don't damage the environment

**toxic**—poisonous

**turbine**—a machine for making electricity with a wheel that's turned by flowing air, steam, or water

**wildfire**—an out-of-control fire in a wild area

# Review and reflect

## COMPREHENSION QUESTIONS

### Fossil fuel frenzy

- What are fossil fuels made from? Why are they considered to be nonrenewable resources?
- What are some of the many uses of fossil fuels?

### Silver linings

- Why would running out of fossil fuels be good news for the environment?
- What are some ways to remove carbon dioxide from the atmosphere?

### Climate complications

- What happens when fossil fuels are burned?
- What happens as a result of global warming?

### Act now

- What are some of the many other alternative energy sources that we can use instead of fossil fuels?
- Solar panels on Earth's surface do not work well on a cloudy day or at night. What is the Iranian American electrical engineer Ali Hajimiri working on to generate solar power 24/7?

### Running low

- Why is fracking controversial?
- Why do some governments allow fracking?

### Conclusion and summary

- After reading this book and considering what would happen if all the fossil fuels ran out, what is your biggest takeaway? Why?

### The end

- What is the first big change we will notice as we run out of fossil fuels?
- What are some ways of making plastics without extracting new fossil fuels?

# MAKE A CHAIN OF EVENTS!

Creating a paper chain can help you explore and visualize how cause and effect relationships can be thought of as a sequence of events.

**You'll need:**
- Pencil
- Scratch paper
- Pens or markers
- Stapler and staples
- Strips of paper (2 colors, if possible)

**Instructions:**

1. **Select a focus:** Choose a specific aspect from the book that caught your attention—it could be how animal remains became something that you use every day, or what life in your community would be like if it switched to an alternative form of energy.

2. **Brainstorm causes and effects:** On a sheet of scratch paper, brainstorm and list the causes and effects related to your chosen focus. Think critically about the factors that contributed to or resulted from your focus. You can always look back in the text for ideas!

3. **Write on strips:** Write each cause and each effect on its own strip of paper. If you have different colored paper, use one color for the cause strips and the other for the effect strips.

4. **Create the paper chain:** Organize your strips into causes and effects. Start forming a paper chain to show how a cause leads to an effect. Use the stapler to connect the two strips. Continue adding cause and effect strips as links in your chain. When you've finished, you should be able to start at the beginning of your chain and read through each chain link in a logical order.

5. **Linking multiple chains:** If your focus has multiple causes or effects, you can create additional chains and link them together to show how complex cause and effect relationships can be!

## Write about it!

Look at the paper chain you created and how the causes link to effects (which in turn link to other causes!). How might breaking a link in the chain impact the overall sequence of events?

World Book, Inc.
180 North LaSalle Street
Suite 900
Chicago, Illinois 60601
USA

For information about other World Book publications, visit our website at www.worldbook.com or call 1-800-WORLDBK (967-5325).

For information about sales to schools and libraries, call 1-800-975-3250 (United States), or 1-800-837-5365 (Canada).

Library of Congress Control Number: 2024941780

What Would Happen If...
ISBN: 978-0-7166-7125-1 (set, hard cover)

All the Fossil Fuels Ran Out?
ISBN: 978-0-7166-7127-5 (hard cover)
ISBN: 978-0-7166-7139-8 (e-book)
ISBN: 978-0-7166-7133-6 (soft cover)

# Staff

**Editorial**

Vice President
Tom Evans

Editorial Project Coordinator
Kaile Kilner

Curriculum Designer
Caroline Davidson

Senior Editor
Shawn Brennan

Proofreader
Nathalie Strassheim

**Graphics and Design**

Senior Visual
Communications Designer
Melanie Bender

Digital Asset Specialist
Rosalia Bledsoe

Written by Izzi Howell
Illustrated by Paula Bossio

Developed with World
Book by White-Thomson
Publishing LTD

# Acknowledgments

4-5 © Andrzej Polak, Shutterstock; © noPPonPat/Shutterstock
6-7 © Mark Agnor, Shutterstock; © Oil and Gas Photographer/Shutterstock
8-9 © Ded Mityay, Shutterstock; © Gary Whitton, Shutterstock; © Vitalii Stock/Shutterstock; © j.chizhe/Shutterstock; © Mouse family/Shutterstock
10-11 © koya979/Shutterstock; © Loredana Sangiuliano/Shutterstock
12-13 © Mizzick/Shutterstock; © Kodda/Shutterstock
14-15 © Brarymi/Alamy Images; © Georgette Apol, Alamy Images
16-17 © J. G. Domke/Alamy Images; © Madeleine Jettre, Alamy Images
18-19 © Victor St. John, Alamy Images; © Troutnut/Shutterstock
20-21 © Cynthia Lee, Alamy Images; © Sipa US/Alamy Images
22-23 © My Portfolio/Shutterstock; © 4045/Shutterstock

24-25 © Pramote Polyamate, Alamy Images; © Quang Ngo, Alamy Images
28-29 © Orjan Ellingvag, Alamy Images; © Dragon Images/Shutterstock
30-31 © Piyaset/Shutterstock; © Rich Carey, Shutterstock
32-33 © luca pbl/Shutterstock; © Helene ROCHE Photography/Alamy Images
34-35 © Kletr/Shutterstock; © Evgeny_V/Shutterstock; © Fokke Baarssen, Shutterstock
36-37 © Constantine Androsoff, Shutterstock; © Diyana Dimitrova, Shutterstock; © engel.ac/Shutterstock; © Fokke Baarssen, Shutterstock
38-39 © imageBROKER.com GmbH & Co. KG/Alamy Images; © Petair/Shutterstock
40-41 © j.chizhe/Shutterstock; © Jian Fan, Alamy Images

www.ingramcontent.com/pod-product-compliance
Lightning Source LLC
Chambersburg PA
CBHW060857090426
42737CB00023B/3480